TOUCHPOINTS

Peter Burgham

First Printing: 2021

ISBN 978-1-9196018-2-3   (paperback)

Published by: Peter Burgham
                 York, England

A CIP catalogue record for this book is available from the British Library.

Website: www.burg34.com

Front Cover: Glen Nevis, Scotland
Back Cover: Woodland walk, Yorkshire

*Dedicated to my wife
and our family and friends
with love*

Contents

Enigma of the Glen

Here at the commotion of opposites
at the Cell Tower Intersection of 3 Cells
invisible inaudible intangible
remote

where Science and Superstition
and the Assemblies of the Celestial
endlessly swirl and agitate

where Wisdom prevails over Opinion
and Patience quiets the raging Wind
where Honesty roots out Greed and Envy
and the Power of Love
transcends the Love of Power
where Time is past and present
    yet briefly absent

here unseen is a spectral storm
    of Protons and Electrons
    of Sorcery and Legend
    secret Paths and silent Talk
here for a moment we touch

The Allerton Oak

A child lifts a fallen acorn,
looks in awe at the noble tree
holding sway like a sceptred earl,
and eagerly bags the woodland pearl.

The mighty oak's borne witness
from badger's snout & squirrel's paw
to the hundred trials of swains & lords,
the king's decrees and clash of swords.

A legend for all seasons, survivor
of storms and wars and the shipman's axe,
of mildew, moths and ordnance blast,
with epic tales of the millennium past.

And now before the court the child
swears solemn oath upon the seed,
while propped by guardians all around
the gnarled old oak defends its ground.

** *The Allerton Oak is a celebrated thousand-year-old tree in Calderstones Park, Liverpool.*

Friendship

Walking together to the pier's end
sharing a dram of coastal air.

Listening with a shell to our ear
we smile at its tale of the sea.

We build memories with sandcastles
and fly kites that touch the sky.

Nothing is left on the beach
except our footprints.

Catching the blue and breezy white
we sight as well the looming grey.

When it's dark and all is shadow
we hold hands and count the stars.

We're seagulls skimming the waves,
dancing wing to wing.

Châteaucreux

A rainbow cut
to shards
gems sparkling
in a kaleidoscope

of plexiglass
and steel,
feu de joie
over monochrome.

A *faux-semblant*
an eye-catcher
to gift
the traveller

a chance moment
to pause
the greyscale
journey.

Behind the Glass

We taste the ruby
scent the blue

raise the mainsail
set our course

leave city stripes
behind closed doors

Rhapsody in Steel

Colossal spirit of the age of Empire,
with ghosts and whistles of trains
long since spotted,
billowing and thundering
in the mesh of girders,
iron-clad dark chargers
champing through the buffeting
swirl of winds and sepia mist,
the Bridge enduring
the dour tetchy Forth,
an industrial diamond
matchless in its prime,
braw vision of the Victorian railway man,
perfectly blending
the art with the artisan,
a showcase all spick and span
before the inevitable grime,
its patched-up wounds
a bell-toll in the fog for every worker lost,
the legend forged from sweat & tears & myriad
paint schemes endlessly enacted,
heaving to the last wire,
engine of creation,
                  Poetry in Steel.

Lost In Transit

She sits alone
in the waiting-room,
crossword left with
unanswered clues,
peers up at the board,
sighs at the further delay,
nudges her suitcase
into a makeshift footrest,
sips her latte, gone cold,
carries on reading the novel
about an encounter
on a steam train
that became a love affair.

Glancing again
at the board, she sighs,
sips her cold latte,
sprays a little perfume
on her neck, and in the mist
pictures her Senior Railcard,
left by mistake in her car.
Or was it a taxi ?
No matter, she reasoned,
today is Swansday,
all travel is free.

That's when they found her.
A neighbour had seen her
getting on a bus.

Silver Song

The watchman locks up the scrapyard,
heads for home past the cathedral's
blue cantilever stand.

Birds line the roof,
chanting vespers. Darkness falls.
On the street the dispossessed

wander, tense as steel,
scouring the gutters for silver,
the end of the lane for copper.

Graffiti on the walls
screams
for the love of God.

The river flows on,
the stone
forever still.

Circle of Life

Catch the beauty of a hummingbird
let it slip beneath your surface
cast away the mantle of your pain.

Let the feathered iridescence
of amethyst ruby and emerald illuminate
your grey skies like a jewelled rainbow.

Let the small seeds
spread on your offered palm
be the weight of your world.

Minster Haiku

There's no outsiders
only brothers & sisters
all are welcome here.

Embrace the spirit
the stone & the sainted glass
the quire and the rose.

Ask the big questions
take time for contemplation
seek and find your peace.

Admit your true self
help the weary traveller
turn lost into found.

Let this survivor
show you the light from the dark
guide you on your way.

Sad Shires

(i.m. Wilfred Owen)

In a year when sinister smoke filled the sky,
When, despite what you saw, did you understand why ?
As you charged through the valleys of death in the shires,
With pointing of fingers and screeching of tyres,
At the dawning of the two-car Age,
Into the new Millennium with the same old Rage,
In the midst of the phoney fast-lane battle,
What passing horns were sounded for those dying cattle ?
What lights for the burning fields and the rotting piles ?
What thoughts beyond the guy ahead & business miles?

In a year when sinister smoke filled the sky,
When the new world shook, when we saw so many die,
As the agents of death charged through skyscraper valleys,
When fingers were pointed at the wailing disease,
At the dawning of the new crusade,
Into the new Apocalypse rattling the same old blade,
In the midst of the cries of infidel and vengeance,
What bells were tolled for the passing of innocence ?
Did you spare a thought for the world today,
As you cursed the people who got in your way ?

Passage

Cloudless January sky,
bitter wind over frozen lakes.

A jet trail piercing the sky
like a smoking arrow.

You adjust the pillow,
flick through the in-flight movies.

The plain ready meal
a long way from Silvio's.

From your window seat
a blanket of white.

Wedged in by snores,
you ponder the turbulence ahead.

*

The contrail vanishes
into the pale blue.

Later you'll pass beyond
sheets of ice, an iceberg maybe.

Then it's New York,
starting over.

A hiker alone
in the urban forest.

*

The blizzards were harsh
in New York this year.

Big snow, so take care,
wrap up well.

Take comfort
from the gritters.

Message

My footsteps crush
the shell of snow.

The yellow gritbox
a long haul today.

Clouds of frost breath
rise and dwell.

My shovel grates
on concrete grey.

Summer at Silvio's
a distant echo.

All footprints in time
will fade away.

Rambling the Ginnels

each path we take
each turn we make

each mile we go
each smile we show

each hand we lend
each tear we mend

each cross we bear
each load we share

                    in life's gigantic
                    crowded maze

                    it's good to find
                    the snickelways

** *'Ginnels' (also called 'snickelways') are shortcut paths between the houses of a town or village, notably in Yorkshire.*

Sound of Silence

No cars no trucks no background hum
as quiet as a solemn prayer
the end & dawn of a millennium
a thousand dreams dispersed into the air
        the hope for peace to come.

No barking dogs or neighbour's phone
the stillness of the desert
a thousand years now set in stone
all earthly clamour on pause & divert
        this silent world's a megaphone.

Family & Friends

Waiting for the hearse, the mourners
adrift in a fog of solemn thoughts
held back the tears.

Celebration of his life would come later,
the effervescent character, the laughter,
the parties and practical jokes,
a champagne fountain of memories.

For now, the comfort of old familiar faces,
firm handshakes and compassionate hugs.
The ritual wrapped around them
like a warm coat on a winter's day.

He arrived suddenly, unannounced,
swept through the front door,
an apparition. That nose, those ears,
that shock of white hair. The gasps were audible,
like the audience in a magician's show,
seeing a rabbit pulled from a hat. A giant white
rabbit on its hind legs, holding out its paw.

Cousin Matthew's mouth gaped open,
mirrored by his son Mark. Aunt Mary hid
behind Joseph, and even he had a double-take,
remembering his old friend's fondness for pranks,
but jeez this was a stunt too far.
The apparition spoke. Mary shrieked,
Grandma fainted.

It had been many years since Andrew,
the elder brother, had been home from overseas.
Nothing much has changed, he thought,
they're still all as mad as rabbits.

Lunchtime in the City of Kafka

*(on seeing an acrobat walking a tightrope strung high between two tall
buildings in the Old Town Square in Prague)*

the boss
wants us to take the shortest route
between our third-floor offices
either side of the square
we see his logic
efficiency productivity time
makes sense
it's a step in the right direction

Sermon

This spire blessed
with a bygone miracle,
this steadfast chronicler
of parish life, stalwart
guardian of faith, hope
and charity, this green
forever England, this
gently ticking clock.

Yet in modern times
which forsaken corner
desperate for a miracle
would not hope to see
its online order
promising delivery today
instead of the usual
'out-of-stock' ?

Sometimes We Lose Touch

We scent the spice of the island
    city noise is a distant horn
    headlines crackle and fade

a bird sings her news
from the dome of an abandoned
    telephone box

then in a breath is gone

      like a ship that has slipped
        below the horizon

      her voice trailing
        into the ocean gyre.

The old salts mend their sails
    and cast their lines

        whilst for a song we buy
        a little can of island air.

The Drone of the Bees

There was no breeze. A cluster of blackbirds swooped low across the golden glinting fields seeking a late supper. High cirrus trailed rose-pink against the pastel blue evening sky, rabbits scurried past butterflies hustling in the hedgerows, a bank vole scampered across a ditch, the bees droned out their late shift amongst the brambles.

Devilhorn Ridge, they called it, a gentle meadow sheared by a limestone cliff, sinister as a vortex in a placid sea.

He stood alone at the edge, silently staring at the rocks below. Twenty-five years spun into an hour, hanging on the thread of a split-second.

The bowing sun paid its last respects to the day, the butterflies withdrew to quiet nooks, the birds regrouped on high branches, the rabbits and voles sought the soft sanctuary of the burrow, the bees hummed their evensong. Darkness draped the hedges, and the forest settled to the rustling of the night.

*

He was an hour late for work. The night shift banter was droll and relentless. Old hands taking a rise out of the new kid. It was a formality that his pay would be docked, there'd be a reprimand too. 'Hope she was worth it, Jimmy mate.'

Matter-of-fact he said he'd been standing on the Devilhorn for a while, just himself, just for a while.

The room fell as silent as the works clock, high on the wall.

So many questions, Jim …

Delphinium
(after Ted Kooser)

The flowers have withered in this cemetery
in Red Barn Creek where once they framed
the path with hummingbirds hovering
like a line of rifles forming a guard of honor
for the mourners and the passing coffin.

In the distance a train whistle repeats,
sending its condolence on the wings of larks
across the bowing wheatfields of Nebraska,
beyond the faded orange and purple delphi
to the steps of the church.

Hailstones descend on the flowers
strewn like weary old soldiers
awaiting their turn to shake
the dead hand of the frost.

Pause and Rewind

(after W.H. Auden)

Rewind all the clocks, pause the TV
Wipe out the cache of your old memory
Silence the ringtone and text message beep
Bring out the skip, pile your junk in a heap.

Let faxes have their final rattle
Dot matrix prints have one more battle
Tie brown ribbons round the Yellow Pages
Wait for instant photos, arriving in stages.

They were the pioneers, our superheroes,
Changed the world with their ones and zeroes,
Punched holes in cards and printed our bums,
Made our disks floppy, and baffled our Mums.

Not wanted now, like gaslamps and cobblestones,
Pack up the CDs, dismantle the pay phones,
Throw away the maps and the lava lighting
Scribble one last time in *joined-up handwriting.*

We're back to the future anytime soon
Wondering how they ever got a man on the moon.
Hush all the clocks, pause the TV,
And spare a last thought for Old Technology.

*** With due respect to W.H. Auden ('Stop all the clocks') and Roger McGough ('Stop all the cars')*

Busy Important

Ah sorry to hear you're too busy
to collect your child,
due to an important meeting.
I understand.
I used to be busy and important too.
But then they had to let me go, after 20 years.
With regret, they said.

So I went elsewhere to be
busy and important, in a place with
lots of other busy important people.
Then they merged with another company
and they felt it would be in my best interests
to further my career elsewhere.
With regret, they said.

So I became
busy and important elsewhere,
until new young management
came in and decided the time was right
to offer me the opportunity
to retire.
With regret, they said.

And now I'm retired
and still busy
and, if you ask me,
still important,
especially in my new life
as a taxi driver.
No regrets, I said.

Within Touching Distance

The moon, they said   and Mars
The first kiss together   under the stars

The switch on the wall   the child on tip toe
The winners' medals   seconds to go

The heartfelt hugs   at the end of lockdown
The forgiving smile   at the end of a frown

The elusive cure   for #any_disease
The fresh and pure   of a summer breeze

That freefall
moment
when

the space between us
vanishes
into

a kaleidoscope of
infinite
permutations

and nothing is
ever
the same again

Et Cetera

Nobody wants it
        it's not welcome
the long and the short of it
        it just isn't good enough

William didn't say
        I wandered lonely et cetera
Dylan didn't say
        Rage etc against the dying etc
Robert didn't say
        Two roads diverged etc etc

It's the last little boy
to be picked for football
in the school playground

the one with the funny name
and the hand-me-down clothes
and the distant gaze

who wanders alone
and rages inside
and ends up on the wrong path

et cetera
etc etc etc

** *With due acknowledgement here of course to William Wordsworth,
Dylan Thomas and Robert Frost and their famous poems.*

ACKNOWLEDGEMENTS

Some of the verses have been published as part of the series of photo-poems by the same author:

PAUSE AND REWIND

Previously published in '*Tribute Night at the Social*':

Delphinium
Sad Shires
Circle of Life (a variation)
Silver Song   (a reworking of '*Armpit Lane*')

Other Collections by the same author:

BIRD'S EYE VIEW
(anthology including many prize-winning and commended poems, recommended by New Writing North, Sept 2021)

TRIBUTE NIGHT AT THE SOCIAL
(3rd prize, Yeovil Writing Without Restrictions Competition, 2017)

WHISPER ON THE SHORE

Many thanks to the members of **York Writers' Group** for their thoughtful and constructive comments.

More poetry and verse and links to other creative arts can be found on:

www.burg34.com

Disclaimer: There is no endorsement or criticism implied with regards anywhere, anything or anyone mentioned in this book.

The names 'Devilhorn Ridge', 'Red Barn Creek' and 'Silvio's' are entirely fictional.

9 781919 601823